Deep Meditation

–

Pathway to Personal Freedom

Yogani

From The AYP Enlightenment Series

AYP Publishing

For ordering information go to:

www.advancedyogapractices.com

Library of Congress Control Number: 2005936614

Published simultaneously in:

Nashville, Tennessee, U.S.A.
and
London, England, U.K.

This title is also available in eBook format – ISBN 0-9764655-5-8
(For Adobe Reader)

ISBN 0-9764655-4-X (Paperback)

"Be still, and know that I am God..."

Psalm 46:10

Introduction

The Advanced Yoga Practices Enlightenment Series is an endeavor to present the most effective methods of yoga in a series of easy-to-read books that anyone can use to gain practical results immediately and over the long term. For centuries, these powerful practices have been taught in secret, mainly in an effort to preserve them. Now we find ourselves in the *information age*, and able to preserve knowledge for present and future generations like never before. The question remains: "How far can we go in effectively transmitting spiritual methods in writing?"

Since its beginnings in 2003, the writings of *Advanced Yoga Practices* have been an experiment to see just how much can be conveyed, with much more detail included on practices than in the spiritual writings of the past. Can books provide us the specific means necessary to tread the path to enlightenment, or do we have to surrender at the feet of a *guru* to find our salvation? Well, clearly we must surrender to something, even if it is to our own innate potential to live a freer and happier life. If we are able to do that, and maintain a daily practice, then books like this one can come alive and instruct us in the ways of human spiritual transformation. If the reader is ready and the book is worthy, amazing things can happen.

While one person's name is given as the author of this book, it is actually a distillation of the efforts of thousands of practitioners over thousands of years. This is one person's attempt to simplify and make practical the spiritual methods that many have demonstrated throughout history. All who have gone before have my deepest gratitude, as do the many I am privileged to be in touch with in the present who continue to practice with dedication and good results.

The subject of this volume, *Deep Meditation*, has special significance in the overall list of yoga practices. No other practice can do more to bring us personal freedom in our daily life. The cultivation of our eternal and unshakable inner silence through daily deep meditation has such far-reaching effects that this practice alone is capable of expanding our experience of life to be unending happiness and creativity. That is why I call deep meditation the *heart of yoga*.

I hope you will find this book to be a useful resource as you travel along your chosen path.

Practice wisely, and enjoy!

Table of Contents

Chapter 1 – "Who Am I?"

The most important question we can ask in this life is, "Who am I?" Right after that in importance is the question, "What am I doing here?" Human beings have been asking these two questions since the first thoughts arose in our ancient ancestors. And we are still asking them.

Since the beginning, thousands of years ago, much effort has gone into understanding these basic questions about our humanity and to realizing their implications experientially. "Practices" have been the way by which the experiential component has been cultivated. Chief among practices has been something called "meditation."

Meditation has meant different things to different people. In English dictionaries only a few decades ago, meditation was defined simply as "to think," or "to ponder." Nowadays, there is a deeper understanding, and you can find meditation defined as, "a specific way of thinking that leads to mental, emotional and physical balance." Those with a spiritual bent like to take it a step further, saying that meditation leads us to a direct realization of who we are and what we are doing here. How can this be?

An effective method of meditation leads us to an experience of profound stillness, an inner silence that defies description. It is an emptiness that is full with peace, creativity and happiness. It is the natural condition of our mind beyond the processes of our thinking. We cannot help but get the feeling when we are in this state that this is who we really are. It feels so much like home. It feels so good. It is not only a mental experience. With effective meditation, every cell in our body is brought to a state of profound living stillness. Many of the symptoms of this stillness, this inner silence in our body, are measurable – the whole metabolism slows down along with the mind.

The truly dramatic thing about meditation is not that we can sit down with a mental procedure and have a profound experience of stillness, peace and happiness while meditating. It is much more than that kind of transitory experience, which might be viewed as an escape. Meditation, practiced on a regular basis, cultivates our nervous system to sustain the inner silence experienced while meditating increasingly throughout our daily activity, while we are fully engaged in the world. Not only do we get a glimpse of our "true self" during meditation, but we are also cultivating it as a full time experience in our life. This has huge implications for the quality of our life, with practical benefits reaching into every aspect of our self-perception, relationships and career. While the procedure of meditation can be very pleasurable, the real reason we do it is for the long term benefits in our life. Meditation is a powerful path that leads to personal freedom. Ultimately, meditation answers the two perennial questions:

Who am I? – I am the silent awareness standing behind all this.

What am I doing here? – I am here to grow into full awareness of my true nature, which is peace, creativity and happiness.

Since the beginning, human beings have wondered not only about the true nature of themselves, but also about the nature of the world and cosmos around them. So many mysteries! For thousands of years we have been slowly cracking the codes of *Mother Nature*. Modern applied science provides the most visible evidence of our progress in understanding the workings of our universe. Where we used to ride on horses, now we ride in automobiles, trains and airplanes. Where we used to communicate via messengers on foot, flag-waving and smoke signals, now we send billions of invisible bits of information across the surface of the earth and through the vacuum of outer space. Where we used to experience diseases that periodically threatened the very survival of civilization, now we are able to preempt or quickly cure most illnesses with our rapidly expanding knowledge of bioscience and genetics. It has taken a huge accumulation of knowledge over the centuries to accomplish these things.

In the theoretical science of quantum physics, we have come to the brink of defining the omnipresence and unlimited potential of consciousness itself. It is here that our experience of inner silence rising in meditation intersects with the view that all things are, in fact, the manifestation of one thing – an unbounded field of consciousness. It is only a small step we take in postulating that the unifying essence of all is none other than the living stillness we experience during and after our meditation practice.

This is the ultimate answer to the question, "Who am I?" – I am the essence of everything, and everything that is manifest is the essence of me.

What are the qualities of this so-called unbounded field of consciousness that is behind everything we see? We can find out by practicing meditation. As we experience more of our inner nature through daily meditation, we find that our desires and conduct gradually rise to a higher level than they were before. Our longings become more attuned with an inner unfoldment. No longer do we doubt what we are here for. We come to know that we have come here to live the truth within us in every aspect of our life. No longer do we struggle with moral issues or how we should conduct ourselves in our affairs. We come to know that right action comes from an inner perspective. Love and compassion gradually become the foundation of all that we do. Our actions automatically become harmonizing and unifying in their influence in our life and in the lives of those around us. All of this comes from the practice of effective meditation.

Fortunately, nothing that has been said here so far has to be taken on faith. "Talk is cheap," you know, and results are what will make the difference. Not philosophical arguments. You have heard it all before, yes? We have covered these basics to lay out a rough framework. So now we can move on to something you can get your teeth into, and you can fill in the rest of the picture with your own experience. That is the best approach.

The rest of this book is about the practice of meditation – a highly effective form we call *deep meditation*. With the information that is to follow, you can easily find out what the truth is about meditation, about yourself, and about everything else that is going on around you.

If we follow the simple daily procedure for deep meditation, we will come to know who we are and what we are doing here.

Let's take a closer look…

Chapter 2 – Deep Meditation

The mind is a machine – a thought machine. It produces thoughts all day and throughout much of the night. We experience these endless thoughts in our awareness. The mind itself is not awareness. It is only a machine. We are the awareness. This points to an interesting possibility. If we can bring the thought machine, the mind, to rest, what will we experience? It will be our awareness, our self, minus the incessant activity of the mind. This is what meditation is for, and the consequences of this are far-reaching.

How to Meditate

Deep meditation is a mental procedure that utilizes the nature of the mind to systematically bring the mind to rest. If the mind is given the opportunity, it will go to rest with no effort. That is how the mind works. Indeed, effort is opposed to the natural process of deep meditation. The mind always seeks the path of least resistance to express itself. Most of the time this is by making more and more thoughts. But it is also possible to create a situation in the mind that turns the path of least resistance into one leading to fewer and fewer thoughts. And, very soon, no thoughts at all. This is done by using a particular thought in a particular way. The thought is called a *mantra*.

For our practice of deep meditation, we will use the thought – *I AM*. This will be our mantra.

It is for the sound that we will use *I AM*, not for the meaning of it. The meaning has an obvious significance in English, and *I AM* has a religious meaning in the English Bible as well. But we will not use *I AM* for the meaning – only for the sound. We can also spell it *AYAM*. No meaning there, is there? Only the sound. That is what we want. If your first language is not English, you may spell the sound phonetically in your own language if you wish. No matter how we spell it, it will be the same sound. The power of the sound ...*I AM*... is great when thought inside. But only if we use a particular procedure. Knowing this procedure is the key to successful meditation. It is very simple. So simple that we will devote many pages here to discussing how to keep it simple, because we all have a tendency to make things more complicated. Maintaining simplicity is the key to right meditation.

Here is the procedure of deep meditation: While sitting comfortably with eyes closed, we'll just relax.

We will notice thoughts, streams of thoughts. That is fine. We just let them go by without minding them. After about a minute, we gently introduce the mantra, ...*I AM*...

We think the mantra in a repetition very easily inside. The speed of repetition may vary, and we do not mind it. We do not intone the mantra out loud. We do not deliberately locate the mantra in any particular part of the body. Whenever we realize we are not thinking the mantra inside anymore, we come back to it easily. This may happen many times in a sitting, or only once or twice. It doesn't matter. We follow this procedure of easily coming back to the mantra when we realize we are off it for the predetermined time of our meditation session. That's it. Very simple.

Typically, the way we will find ourselves off the mantra will be in a stream of other thoughts. This is normal. The mind is a thought machine, remember? Making thoughts is what it does. But, if we are meditating, as soon as we realize we are off into a stream of thoughts, <u>no matter how mundane or profound</u>, we just easily go back to the mantra. Like that. We don't make a struggle of it. The idea is not that we have to be on the mantra all the time. That is not the objective. The objective is to easily go back to it when we realize we are off it. We just favor the mantra with our attention when we notice we are not thinking it. If we are back into a stream of other thoughts five seconds later, we don't try and force the thoughts out. Thoughts are a normal part of the deep meditation process. We just ease back to the mantra again. We favor it. Deep meditation is a *going toward*, not a *pushing away from*. We do that every single time with the mantra when we realize we are off it – just easily favoring it. It is a gentle persuasion. No struggle. No fuss. No iron willpower or mental heroics are necessary for this practice. All such efforts are away from the simplicity of deep meditation and will reduce its effectiveness.

As we do this simple process of deep meditation, we will at some point notice a change in the character of our inner experience. The mantra may become very refined and fuzzy. This is normal. It is perfectly all right to think the mantra in a very refined and fuzzy way if this is the easiest. It should always be easy – never a struggle. Other times, we may lose track of where we are for a while, having no mantra, or stream of thoughts either. This is fine too. When we realize we have been off somewhere, we just ease back to the mantra again. If we have been very settled with the mantra being barely recognizable, we can go back to that fuzzy level of it, if it is the easiest. As the mantra refines, we are riding it inward with our attention to progressively deeper levels of inner silence in the mind. So it is normal for the mantra to become very faint and fuzzy. We cannot force this to happen. It will happen naturally as our nervous system goes through its many cycles of *inner purification* stimulated by deep meditation. When the mantra refines, we just go with it. And when the mantra does not refine, we just be with it at whatever level is easy. No struggle. There is no objective to attain, except to continue the simple procedure we are describing here.

When and Where to Meditate

How long and how often do we meditate? For most people, twenty minutes is the best duration for a meditation session. It is done twice per day, once before the morning meal and day's activity, and then again before the evening meal and evening's activity.

Try to avoid meditating right after eating or right before bed. Before meal and activity is the ideal time. It will be most effective and refreshing then. Deep meditation is a preparation for activity, and our results over time will be best if we are active between our meditation sessions. Also, meditation is not a substitute for sleep. The ideal situation is a good balance between meditation, daily activity and normal sleep at night. If we do this, our inner experience will grow naturally over time, and our outer life will become enriched by our growing inner silence.

A word on how to sit in meditation: The first priority is comfort. It is not desirable to sit in a way that distracts us from the easy procedure of meditation. So sitting in a comfortable chair with back support is a good way to meditate. Later on, or if we are already familiar, there can be an advantage to sitting with legs crossed, also with back support. But always with comfort and least distraction being the priority. If, for whatever reason, crossed legs are not feasible for us, we will do just fine meditating in our comfortable chair. There will be no loss of the benefits.

Due to commitments we may have, the ideal routine of meditation sessions will not always be possible. That is okay. Do the best you can and do not stress over it. Due to circumstances beyond our control, sometimes the only time we will have to meditate will be right after a meal, or even later in the evening near bedtime. If meditating at these times causes a little disruption in our system, we will know it soon enough and make the necessary adjustments. The main thing is that we do our best to do two meditations every day, even if it is only a short session between our commitments. Later on, we will look at the options we have to make adjustments to address varying outer circumstances, as well as inner experiences that can come up.

Before we go on, you should try a meditation. Find a comfortable place to sit where you are not likely to be interrupted and do a short meditation, say ten minutes, and see how it goes. It is a toe in the water. Make sure to take a couple of minutes at the end sitting easily without doing the procedure of meditation. Then open your eyes slowly. Then read on here.

As you will see, the simple procedure of deep meditation and it's resulting experiences will raise some questions. We will cover many of them here.

So, now we will move into the practical aspects of deep meditation – your own experiences and initial symptoms of the growth of your own inner silence.

Questions On Your First Meditation

A first meditation is very special. No matter what the experience, our first deep meditation using the *I AM* mantra marks the beginning of new openings of our latent potential. If we continue with our daily meditation practice over months and years, these openings will expand more and more, until our experience of life becomes transformed to permanent peace, creativity and joy.

But, in the beginning, it is all new, and there are many questions that can come up about the process of meditation and the experiences we have. Here are some questions that are often asked after a first meditation:

Is something supposed to happen? Not much did.

No, nothing in particular is supposed to happen. Nothing except following the easy procedure of meditation. That is, easily thinking the mantra and easily picking it back up when we realize we are off into a stream of thoughts.

Experientially, we can have a meditation that is nothing more than that – mantra, thoughts, back to mantra, more thoughts and so on, over and over again. What is not always obvious is that each time we "lose" the mantra, we have gone through a natural shift in our attention. During that shift, there is a space, or gap, between thinking the mantra and then finding ourselves in a stream of thoughts. In that space, we have touched our inner silence, our pure awareness, our inner self. It might not feel that we have touched anything. Yet, the stream of thoughts we experience afterward is a clear sign that we have gone in with the mantra and are coming back out with the habit of the mind to generate thoughts. This cycle of thinking the mantra, losing it, and coming out into a stream of thoughts is a process of purification in the mind and nervous system. It is very powerful, and will ultimately yield a constant experience of inner silence in our meditation and, more importantly, in our daily activity.

It is the twice-daily process of meditation that will produce the results, and our experiences both inside and outside meditation will vary over time. It is the practice that will open us up from within, not any particular experience we might have along the way. For this reason, we sometimes refer to our experiences in meditation as *scenery*. Even uninteresting experiences (not much happening) are the scenery of the mind. When we are driving a car, it is the destination we are moving toward, regardless of the scenery we may pass on the way. The scenery will change as we travel along, and we will be moving closer to our destination with the passage of time. If we are busy driving, or talking with someone who is riding with us, we may not see the scenery out the window, but we will still be moving along toward our destination just the same. Seemingly uneventful meditations are like that. If we are involved in doing the practice, we will be moving swiftly along, whether we are having a lot of noticeable experiences or not.

So if your first meditation seemed a bit uneventful, take heart! Good things are happening when we follow the procedure. The best indication of progress in meditation is in how we feel afterward when we get up and go out into our daily activity. If your first meditation was uneventful, see how you feel in the hours after. Is there some relaxation, some inner calm as you go about your daily activities? That is the real test of meditation.

I felt at one with the blissful cosmos. Was I?

Interestingly, we are always at one with the blissful cosmos. We are all expressions of *That*. The only reason we do not experience this in every moment is because impurities in our nervous system block our perception of the true nature of life. These impurities are gradually dissolved in deep meditation, and then we begin to see the truth of who we are. In our very first meditation we may have a clear experience of our unbounded blissful nature. That is who we are!

What should we do when we have an experience like this in our meditation? The answer is very simple – when we realize we are off into such an experience (no matter how cosmic or glorious) and no longer on the mantra, we easily pick up the mantra again.

Keep in mind that we are involved in a process of purification that will likely take many years of daily meditation practice. Our nervous system is the storehouse of eons of impurities and obstructions created by past actions. Our nervous system is also the window through which we can see our true nature and the true nature of all things. As we are cleaning our window bit by bit in deep meditation, the view gradually becomes more clear.

Consider a partly sunny day with many big clouds moving slowly across the sky. Sometimes our view of the sun will be obstructed behind the clouds. Other times the sun will shine brightly on us between the clouds. With deep meditation, we are clearing our inner clouds. Gradually, there will be fewer and fewer clouds blocking our inner light. In time, we will succeed in dissolving all the clouds, so we will be bathed in our inner light throughout the day and night. That is what deep meditation is for, and that is why we always ease back to the mantra when we find that we have drifted off it. We can enjoy our cosmic bliss in meditation when it happens, just as we can enjoy the scenery as we are traveling along on our car journey. But the journey of meditation can only continue if we come back to the mantra, and we should always remember that.

I felt some restlessness, some irritability. Why?

There are many obstructions lodged deep in our nervous system. Meditation loosens and gradually releases these, usually without discomfort. But sometimes there can be a surge of unwinding within us, and there can be some restlessness or irritability along with that surge. It is neurobiological energy moving within us. As we continue with the simple procedure of meditation, the surge and discomfort will pass.

It can also happen that we will feel a surge of pleasurable energy from the same cause – an unwinding of obstructions in our nervous system. In either case, we continue with the procedure of meditation, easily coming back to the mantra when we realize we are off it.

If our experiences in meditation become very strong, making it difficult to continue with comfort, there are things we can do to regulate the inner energy flow. These will be discussed in the next chapter.

The Possibilities

The key to success in deep meditation is steadfast daily practice over the long term. As mentioned, it is not primarily for the experience within meditation that we are doing this. It is for a permanent positive change in the quality of our life. And we will find just that as the weeks, months and years of daily meditation practice go by.

The results can be subtle. Others may notice a change in us before we do. It is common for a family member or friend to comment, "What is going on?

You are much less edgy lately. You haven't lost your temper in weeks."

This is a symptom of inner silence creeping up in us. We begin to see the world from a deeper place within ourselves – a place that is not undone by the daily ups and downs of life. We become more *centered.* Even as life in and around us goes on much as it did before, we are somehow different. The stresses and strains of life begin to lose their grip on us. Besides the obvious mental and physical health benefits, this rise of inner silence is very liberating and frees us to express ourselves in ways that might not have been possible before.

Increased creativity is one of the benefits of rising inner silence. It is well known that great geniuses throughout history have received their inspirations when in states of mental relaxation. Their revelations often came from "out of nowhere." Deep meditation in our daily life naturally leads us to a perpetually more relaxed mind, and to the greater levels of creativity that come with that condition. In that way, we can say that meditation will help us to become more intelligent, simply by giving us better access to the latent genius that lies within us all.

Steadfastness is another trait that comes with rising inner silence. Since we are swayed less by the ups and downs of life, we find ourselves in the position to stand firm in the face of adversity when it is necessary. So too do we become stronger in our moral convictions, and take a greater interest in matters of rightness and truth. With deep meditation, we find that we become morally stronger and, at the same time, more flexible in dealing with the many shades of life we encounter each day.

One of the primary characteristics of the natural morality which emerges from within us as part of our rising inner silence is the quality of *love*. So, while we are becoming more resilient, creative and strong, we are also becoming more caring and compassionate. Our ability to give expands, because we have more available within ourselves.

All of these qualities rise naturally by engaging in daily deep meditation, which purifies our nervous system so our latent divine nature can begin to express through us.

In addition to the many practical benefits deep meditation can bring us in daily life, we also can find ourselves opening in ways that reach far beyond anything we could have imagined. This brings us to consider the possibility of *enlightenment*. In fact, if we take the benefits we have mentioned so far, and take them to their highest level of expression, we arrive at something quite remarkable. That something is none other than the condition of human spiritual transformation that has been described by saints and sages throughout history, beginning with the first spiritual writings thousands of years ago.

What is enlightenment? In its most basic form, it is abiding inner silence. It is directly and automatically experiencing who and what we are in every moment – while we are awake, while we are in dreaming sleep, and while we are in dreamless deep sleep. Always aware, always awake inside. That is the possibility that deep meditation puts before us.

From this basic form of enlightenment, we find additional possibilities as our unshakable inner silence expresses further within us, and outward into the surrounding environment. In this way are we able to bring much good into the world, simply by living our everyday life in a state of perpetual personal freedom.

Chapter 3 – Steps of Progress

Now that we have covered the essentials of deep meditation practice, let's look further into the processes that are at work within us. It will be good to understand the mechanics of our practice in relation to the various things that are going on in our nervous system. With a good understanding of the symptoms of purification and also the more glamorous experiences that might come up, we will be in the best position to maintain our practice over the long term. No matter what our experiences may be today, tomorrow or the next day, it will be long term daily deep meditation practice that will determine our results more than any other factor.

The many experiences we have along the way, combined with the means we use to navigate through our daily meditation practice, will form the steps of progress we go through in cultivating permanent inner silence within us, and the freedom it will bring in all aspects of our life.

Navigating the Path of Inner Purification

We have already mentioned three basic possibilities of experience that we might have in our first meditation – "Not much happening," "Cosmic bliss!" and "Restlessness." All of these are symptoms of purification occurring deep within our nervous system. We already know that in any of these cases, we just easily come back to the mantra when we realize we are not on it anymore. No strain. No fuss. It is just a simple procedure.

Yet, we all have an amazing ability to become fascinated or otherwise focused on the musings of our mind, the longings of our heart, the sensations in our body, and the sensory inputs from our surroundings. Indeed, such experiences are the things that keep us going through life, and they are completely natural. Yet, in deep meditation we are doing something quite different, and that is the crucial difference between deep meditation and most everything else we are doing in our life.

In daily life, the activities of the mind, heart and body are the things we act upon. In deep meditation, we develop the habit of letting them all go in favor of the mantra. This process of repeatedly letting go of everything that comes up during meditation in favor of the mantra causes an amazing transformation to occur in us. This transformation is a process of *purification and opening*. We come to know this process quite well in deep meditation, operating by the unique procedure. In deep meditation, we are operating in a different mode in relation to thoughts, feelings and sensations than we do in our daily activity. They might even be the same kinds of thoughts, feelings and sensations. Yet, we treat them in a different way during deep meditation.

Taken all together, these thoughts, feelings and sensations we experience in deep meditation are called *symptoms of purification*. While many of these are routinely handled by easily coming back to the mantra, some of our experiences will need additional instructions for us to handle them in deep meditation. Sometimes we can experience symptoms of purification while we are engaged in our daily activities too, and these may also require some additional instructions, which will be included here as well.

A closer look at symptoms of purification and situations we may encounter during or after our meditation are included here, along with guidelines on how to handle them.

Persistent Thoughts – Mantra is Hard to Pick Up

It has been mentioned that thoughts are a natural product in deep meditation – a symptom of purification in our nervous system. While it may feel like an ordinary thought process we are having, it is not, as long as we are following the procedure of meditation.

So, if we sit to meditate, and after about a minute pick up the mantra one time and go off into an endless stream of thoughts for the rest of the session, this is a good meditation. If we notice we are off the mantra, we will easily come back to it, right? But if we do not notice during the long and persistent thought stream, and it goes on to the end of the session like that, it is fine. A lot of purification is going on. When our time is up, we take our rest for a few minutes, get up and go out into activity. The result will be more clarity after our meditation.

If we find ourselves off into a stream of thoughts and realize we are off the mantra, our procedure is to easily come back to the mantra. Sometimes, the thoughts can be so continuous, or forceful, that we do not find the mantra coming easily. Or if it does come, it is drowned out by the powerful thought stream immediately. More purification! It is important not to strain against this. We could wind up with a headache if we force it. Neither do we try and analyze the content of the thought stream.

If the mantra does not come easily, or is drowned out by a powerful thought stream immediately when we pick it up, we just take it easy. If it seems difficult or hard to pick up the mantra, we just don't do it. Instead, we relax and let the powerful thought stream go on for a while, just easily observing without engaging in the content of it, or judging it in any way. When we do this benign observation of a powerful thought stream, we will find that it will dissipate after a few minutes. Then we can easily pick up the mantra again and continue. All of this is part of the process of meditation. In this way we can navigate through a release, a process of purification that manifested itself as an intense stream of thoughts.

There will be times when such a symptom of purification will persist through an entire meditation, and sometimes through several meditation sessions. It is rare that it will happen like that, but it can happen. In that case we just continue following the procedure of our meditation, adding the above measure as necessary. Sooner or later the obstructions behind the release will dissolve and we will see more clarity in our meditation. Even if there are endless thoughts in our meditation, we should notice more clarity in our daily activity, because there is much purification going on during our meditation. Always make sure to take at least a few minutes of rest at the end of deep meditation, without any favoring of the mantra, before opening the eyes and getting up. This will allow any residual purification occurring in the meditation to unwind, so we will be smooth in our daily activity.

Thoughts and Mantra Together

It is common to have several things going on at the same time in meditation. For example, we can easily be thinking the mantra, and be having thought streams coming up at the same time. We can have thoughts and mantra at the same time. What do we do in this situation?

It is the same procedure. We just easily favor the mantra. If other thoughts are there, that is okay. We don't try to get rid of them. Neither do we embrace them, no matter how profound they might seem. Gradually they will dissipate as the underlying obstructions in our nervous system are released. As long as we follow the procedure of favoring the mantra when we realize we are off it, then the process of inner purification will continue.

In some cultures, mantras are used in the background of the mind constantly in daily activity, always going on with whatever the people are doing. Deep meditation is not like that. It is a specific practice we sit and do twice per day, letting go of all else. Then we go out into our daily life and forget about meditation and the mantra. Whatever our life is in daily activity, that is what we do. This is mentioned because sometimes when people with a "mantra habit" learn deep meditation, they think that engaging in regular thought processes with the mantra in the background will be the same as deep meditation. It is not. Deep meditation can only be deep meditation if we are easily favoring the mantra over other thought processes whenever we realize we are not with the mantra. So, deliberately going through the grocery list in our mind while repeating the mantra in the background is not deep meditation. If we have the grocery list in the mind and we easily go to the mantra whenever we realize we are not doing that, then this is deep meditation. It is a fine point, and a very important one.

When we have both thoughts and mantra in the mind during our meditation, as long as we are favoring the mantra when we see we are off it, we will be in deep meditation. If we are favoring the thoughts, even though we know we can favor the mantra, that is not deep meditation. The difference in results between these two approaches is profound.

So, thoughts and mantra are okay, and it will happen. Just easily favor the mantra, no matter what is going on. Don't force the mantra. We just come back to it every time we remember we are off it. In time, this simple procedure becomes a habit, so whenever we sit down to meditate we go deep into our silence, whether thoughts are present or not. It is this cultivation of inner silence that brings us great freedom in life.

No Mantra, No Thoughts

Sometimes when we are meditating, we will realize that we were off somewhere, not in thoughts, or with the mantra, and not unconscious either. This is not the kind of thing we can ponder while it is happening, because there were no thoughts while it was happening. As soon as we recognize we were there, we are not there anymore. This experience of no mantra and no thoughts can leave us with a feeling of pleasantness, lightness, or euphoria. It is inner silence – pure bliss consciousness. When it happens to us the first few times, we may be tempted to stop and celebrate it, or analyze it. That is fine, but to do so is a diversion from our meditation. So what do we do? We know, right? When we realize we are off celebrating or analyzing, we just easily go back to the mantra. If we are still settled, the mantra may be easy to pick up in a very refined and fuzzy way. Clear pronunciation is not a requirement in deep meditation. The deeper we are, the fuzzier the mantra will be, and along with this we may feel expansion inside, or the sort of no mantra, no thoughts experience mentioned above. On the other hand, we may find ourselves back out in lots of thoughts again. This is a normal process in meditation – more purification going on. We never try to regulate the experience we are having. Deep meditation is not about regulating experiences. It is about following the simple procedure of the practice, no matter what the experience may be.

We might feel a twinge of regret to be back out in thoughts again. It is normal to long for that deep "no mantra, no thoughts" kind of experience. We'd all like to spend all of our meditations immersed in the depths of our blissful silent being. We will certainly have many tastes of that along the way, and it will gradually increase to become a full-time experience over many months and years of daily practice. Eventually our entire life will be filled with that unshakable inner silence that we taste when we are in deep meditation. And that is why we meditate – to improve the quality of our daily life over the long term.

If we get attached to the peak experiences that we will inevitably have in deep meditation, and make them a goal when we sit to meditate, this will not be helpful to our process. It is not reasonable to expect that we will have profound experiences in every meditation. There is too much housecleaning to be done. Make no mistake about it. When we are meditating we are doing a long term deep housecleaning of our nervous system, and the dust will fly in the form of thoughts, feelings and sensations. It is in-between the dust flying that we will have glimpses of our inner nature. So, if we have a goal for a particular experience in meditation, we will surely be disappointed. The correct way is to let it go and just follow the easy procedure, no matter what else happens. Doing this, whatever experience we may have in meditation, we will find the best results in our daily activity. How we feel *after meditation* is the best measure of the success of our practice – not the ups and downs of our experiences in deep meditation, which is only the housecleaning. Deep meditation is not an end in itself. It is the preparation for a life in freedom.

Breath Slowing Down

When our mind settles down during deep meditation, the body naturally goes with it. This can be measured directly in a variety of our biological functions. One of these is the breath, which is tied to our rate of metabolism. So, mind slows down, energy consumption in the body slows down, metabolism in our cells slows down, and breath slows down.

In fact, sometimes, breath can practically stop during our deep meditation. This is nothing to worry about. It means that our body is going to profound levels of quietness during meditation, and this is the catalyst for deep purification within our nervous system. So, the breath slowing down in deep meditation is a precursor of purification in the nervous system, a natural manifestation of the presence of inner silence.

It is very revealing that the breath slows down automatically as the mind goes to stillness. It is direct proof of the intimate mind/body connection that exists in us. We don't need a laboratory experiment to verify this. All we have to do is sit and meditate, and we will see for ourselves soon enough.

We do not make an effort to slow the breath while we are meditating. Neither do we deliberately synchronize the mantra with the breath. If it happens inadvertently, it is okay, but we do not favor it. We just leave the breath to do naturally what it will in deep meditation. This is how we will achieve the best results. Deep meditation is just a simple procedure of easily favoring the mantra, no matter what else may come to our attention – breath, thoughts, feelings, physical sensations, and so on. In our practice of deep meditation, less will be more and more will be less. While other systems of practice may use the breath as an object of attention, we do not in deep meditation.

It is by following the procedure of deep meditation that the process of purification will be conducted automatically in our nervous system. Sometimes the mind will go very still, and usually the breath along with it. Other times we will be filled with thoughts and sensations inside, and the breath will be normal. It is even possible for the breath to speed up for short periods if the body is undergoing strong purification. But the more common experience will be a slowing down of the breath. It is normal, and part of the beneficial effects of deep meditation.

Physical Discomfort, Pain or Restlessness

We have already mentioned "restlessness" in discussing the possible range of experiences that may have come up in our first meditation. We all react a little differently to deep meditation, depending on the matrix of obstructions that is lodged deep in our nervous system. Also, everyone will experience variations in experiences over time. Today we may be deep in silence during meditation. Tomorrow, lots of thoughts will be coming up. The next day, there could be some restlessness. And so on…

What will be a constant as we continue with our practice will be the steady rise of inner silence in the midst of our daily activities, regardless of the ups and downs of inner purification we will be experiencing within our meditation sessions. Having this understanding enables us to continue with our daily practice through all the peaks, valleys and plateaus we will encounter along the road to personal freedom. Few paths go in a straight line, and the path of deep meditation is no exception.

Along the way, most of us are bound to experience the sort of mild irritability discussed in the last chapter. When we do, we just regard it as any other thought or sensation that may come, and easily favor the mantra.

A few of us may experience more acute physical discomfort from time to time in the form of extreme restlessness, or even pain somewhere in the body. If any such sensation comes up and we find we are unable to easily return to the mantra, then we just let go of the process and let our attention reside with the discomfort we feel inside. Our attention will naturally be drawn to the area of discomfort. When it is, we just let it reside there without judging or focusing on the sensation. We let the attention be there naturally. If the discomfort is due to inner purification it will often unwind within a few minutes. After it does, we will be able to easily pick up the mantra again and continue our meditation. The time we spend letting our attention be with discomfort counts as part of our total meditation time. So, if our regular meditation time is twenty minutes, and we spend ten minutes of that letting our attention be on a particular area of discomfort, that is okay. The purification will still be going on.

In the event of a physical injury or condition we may have that can cause some discomfort in meditation, the first priority will be to find a comfortable seat. If sitting up straight in a chair is not comfortable, we can lean back on a pile of pillows on the bed. If that is not going to be comfortable, we can lie down. However, lying down is not the preferred position for deep meditation if we are able to sit up comfortably. Lying down and meditating is better than being very uncomfortable sitting up, or not meditating at all. However, lying down during meditation does increase the chance of falling asleep during the session. We'd like for the mind to be reasonably alert for meditation, allowing us to conduct the simple procedure that can bring us so much benefit. So sitting up comfortably is the preferred position.

As for physical discomfort we might bring on ourselves during meditation by trying to sit in a position or posture we are not accustomed to, this is something we should minimize as much as possible.

The mythological figure meditating in a pretzel posture on a hard rock with no back support, is just that – a mythological figure. Not a practical everyday meditator like you and me. Let's be comfortable. We do not have to be sphinx-like in our sitting. If we have an itch, we can scratch. If our body wants to stretch during meditation, we can do that. As always, we just easily come back to the mantra.

Strong Emotions

Just as purification can manifest itself in thoughts or physical sensations, it can also manifest in our emotions. We might be sitting there in deep meditation, having a stream of thoughts coming up. Just as we are picking up the mantra again, we might begin to feel very emotional about some thought, or maybe about nothing in particular – just a strong feeling coming out of nowhere. Or we could feel very excited about something we sensed in our meditation, only to find later on that we were very excited about something as mundane as some mush we stepped in. Or we could get very angry about something while in meditation, only to find when we come out that the anger is gone, and we don't even remember what we were angry about deep in the recesses of our mind and nervous system.

These kinds of emotional experiences that can come up in meditation are symptoms of purification. When they do come up, and we remember we are off the mantra, we just easily come back to it. If the emotions are so strong that we cannot easily pick up the mantra, then we follow the procedure discussed before, where we just let the attention reside with the sensation of the emotion. Usually this will aid in its unwinding. Once it lets up, we can go back to easily picking up the mantra for the rest of our meditation time. Then we will feel much clearer in activity, because something has been released deep within us.

Interestingly, there will often be a physical correspondence somewhere in the body with strong emotions we have in meditation. When we are not able to easily go back to the mantra, and let our attention reside with a strong emotion, we will usually be drawn to a physical location in the body where the unwinding of the inner obstruction is occurring. So there is a close relationship between strong emotions and the inner dynamics within our physical body and nervous system. This is not surprising, of course, and is more evidence of the mind/body connection.

Some in the field of psychology might be tempted to analyze the content of all these emotions that come up during deep meditation, and perhaps even the content of the ordinary thought streams that emerge as we are diving repeatedly into the silent depths of our mind. This is not recommended, as it effectively ends the process of deep meditation. If we are not easily favoring the mantra when we realize we have gone off it, then we are not engaged in deep meditation anymore. Given the benefits gained through inner purification stimulated by the easy process of meditation, it is recommended that all analysis be suspended during our meditation sessions. If there is to be analysis, let it be after our meditation sessions. Then we can analyze to our heart's content without disrupting the process of unfoldment we are stimulating within ourselves during meditation. Also, after meditation, we will be much clearer in our perspective because we will be one meditation session closer to naturally sustaining blissful inner silence throughout our daily life. This is the quality in us that enables us to see things as they really are – thus, increasing our analytical skills profoundly. The best way to increase our analytical skills is to completely forget about analysis during deep meditation!

Headache

If we have brought a headache into our meditation from our daily activity we will often find some relief. This is because deep meditation is one of the best known means for relieving short term and long term causes of stress symptoms within us. Many headaches are in this category. Of course, if a headache is related to a medical condition, we should see a doctor. But, very often, a stress-related headache situation will be relieved in deep meditation, along with many of the other stresses and inner obstructions we have accumulated throughout our life. That is inner purification, which will have a direct positive impact on our overall health.

It is also possible that we can give ourselves a headache in deep meditation. This is nearly always due to some straining in the process of meditation – trying to force the mantra, trying to force out thoughts or feelings, trying to hang on to certain kinds of experiences, and so on. All of these attempts to control the process of meditation cause strain in the mind and nervous system. And the result can be a headache, or other unpleasant symptoms.

It is also possible that we can get a headache in meditation doing the procedure just right, if we hit a patch of heavy purification in the head. It can happen. In that case we follow the procedure for dealing with discomfort in meditation. However, headaches related to purification in meditation are rare. More often, the cause will be that we are forcing something in the meditation procedure. Maintaining the simplicity of our practice is the key.

Falling Asleep in Meditation, or Blackout

Sometimes we may sit to meditate and lose ourselves for a while, only to "wake up" later, feeling groggy, as if from a deep sleep. We may find our head drooped way down on our chest. Were we asleep?

If we seem to be asleep in meditation, we can be sure that it is a special kind of sleep associated with purification going on deep within us. Sometimes we will be conscious throughout the so-called meditative sleep, with no manta and no thoughts. Other times we can be unconscious, so much so that we could describe our experience as being a complete *blackout*.

This sort of experience, a sleep-like state with awareness or with no awareness, can occur in meditation in a single meditation session, or for several sessions in a row. It is the sign of deep purification going on. Once we have gotten through it, we will find ourselves entering the next phase of purification in deep meditation, whatever it may be.

Keep in mind that deep meditation is a housecleaning deep inside our nervous system. In some ways it goes much deeper than the deepest sleep we can have at night. Yet, meditation is not a substitute for sleep. The best all-around routine is one that has good balance between our meditation sessions, our daily activity, and our normal sleep at night. If we begin to do too much or too little of any of these components, we will likely experience some discomfort, some imbalance in our life.

Procedurally, nothing changes if we experience a sleep-like state during deep meditation. When we realize we have been off the mantra, we easily come back to it. We may go off into the sleep state again, or not. The time we spend in this state counts as part of our regular meditation time. If we wake up after our meditation time is up, then we just come out slowly, taking at least a few minutes before getting up, like always.

If we feel groggy at the end of our meditation, it will help to take some extra time coming out. We can lie down for five or ten minutes, or even take a nap if we have time.

If we become so groggy in the middle of our meditation that it is difficult to pick the mantra back up, we can lie down for a while. That sort of lying down also counts as part of our meditation time. If we are able to come back to the mantra again later in our session, it will be good to sit back up again, at least part way, with good back support.

It is possible to have this sort of dullness or sleepiness happening in deep meditation for a series of sessions. And then it will finally clear up. If we are practicing according to the procedures of deep meditation, we should find clarity in our daily activities even while we are having the sleepy meditations.

Take heart! It is all part of the cycles of purification going on deep inside us. In the long run, we will be infused with the bliss of steady state inner silence. All of the ups and downs in practice are leading to that in our daily activity.

External Noise

Certainly no one would want to be meditating with a jack-hammer running right outside the window. On the other hand, it is possible to meditate with that going on – or on airplanes, on buses, on trains, in cars, and even in waiting rooms full of people. How can we meditate in such distracting situations?

Well, it is not our first choice, for sure. Whenever we can find a quiet place to meditate where we will not be distracted, that will be ideal. And if it is not available, we can still meditate with equal effectiveness just about anywhere. This is because the procedure of deep meditation considers all stimuli in the mind exactly the same, including sensory inputs. So we can continue with meditation no matter what our attention is attracted to – thoughts, emotions, physical sensations, noise, flashing lights (outside or inside!) and anything else that may come up. So if we are sitting in meditation and someone starts up the jack-hammer outside our window, no doubt our attention will naturally be drawn to it. When that happens and we realize we are off the mantra, what do we do? Just easily go back to the mantra. The meditation can go on just fine, noise or not. The proof of this will be in our experience. It is a fact that some of the deepest meditations we will ever have will be in circumstances that we never imagined we could even get started meditating, let alone go deep into inner silence.

The truth is that whether we are deep or not in meditation has little to do with the environment we are meditating in. It is much more a function of the cycles of purification occurring in our nervous system. So, the next time you are meditating in a noisy place, keep that in mind and just carry on.

There is something else that should be mentioned about meditation and attention in relation to noise and other sensory stimuli. Over the long term of our daily meditation practice, we will find that inner silence becomes more a resident part of our awareness. We will be naturally more quiet and blissful inside, all the time. As this occurs, our inner silence will be noticed in meditation as an immediately available *charm* in the process of going inward. As soon as we close our eyes, we will go beyond the grip of external stimuli. Indeed, external stimuli will not grab us with eyes open either!

When we have reached this stage, deep meditation will go beyond being a mechanical mental procedure to being more like listening to our favorite music. We will not let go of the procedure of deep meditation. Rather it will merge into the depths of inner silence gradually over time. As this happens, noise and other sensory inputs will have much less effect on our attention in meditation, because we will be naturally attracted to the joyful stillness within. We will hear the noise, but be drawn right back to our inner bliss. The same thing happens in our daily activity when we are not meditating. In this case, all of our activities become infused with the stability, strength and innate love of our inner silence.

So, our life becomes quite joyous, and we become much more effective in living it. So do our meditations gradually become more joyous, whether there is noise around us or not. In the end, all noise is heard within our unshakable inner silence, which is no distraction at all.

Interruptions

What do we do if we are sitting in our room quietly meditating and our Auntie May walks in on us to ask us something?

We can just say, "Auntie May, I am meditating. I'll be with you in twenty minutes."

She will understand and leave us. Then we just easily go back to our meditation. Or, if she says she needs an answer right now, we can give it. In that case, we may be a bit ruffled in our meditation. So we can just relax a minute or two and then start the mantra again. We do not start our time over. In fact, it will be best if we count the interruption time as part of our meditation, like any stream of thoughts, you know.

Now, what if Auntie May runs into the room yelling, "Fire!" What do we do then? Very simple. We get up right away and do whatever is necessary to take care of the situation. The first priority is saving life and limb. In the case where we have to get up and take care of an emergency, we may feel some roughness later on, due to impurities we have left halfway unwound when we jumped up out of our meditation. In that case it will be good to lie down for a while after the emergency has past. Do not start the meditation over. Just take a break and rest when there is an opportunity, and then go back to the next normally scheduled meditation when the appointed time arrives.

As we become more experienced in deep meditation, and have more inner silence residing in our nervous system, then interruptions will be much less intrusive. Like noise and other outside stimuli, interruptions will be found to be happening within our inner silence, more a part of the natural flow of things and no longer an encroachment on us. All of life will become more like that.

Importance of Resting Before Getting up

We have touched several times already on the importance of taking enough rest before getting up from meditation, and it is good to emphasize it again.

Subjectively, there may not seem to be much difference between thoughts and feelings we have inside meditation versus thoughts and feelings we have outside meditation. But there is a huge difference. One of the quickest ways to find this out is to jump up out of meditation with no rest at the end and go straight into activity. It is quite likely that we will become cranky, irritable and downright uncomfortable. We have all done this at one time or other, and it is a good object lesson on the importance of taking proper rest before getting up from our meditation.

When we are in deep meditation, purification is going on deep inside our nervous system. Eons of obstructions are being removed as we plumb the depths of our inner silence. The purpose of rest at the end of our meditation is to allow the releases that are in progress to complete themselves before we get up. This can be as simple as taking a couple of minutes with no mantra while sitting on our meditation seat before we get up, stretching a bit and then slowly opening our eyes. Or, if we have a lot of releases going on in meditation, we may want to lie down for five or ten minutes, and then slowly get up.

The resting stage of our deep meditation is as important as the meditation itself. Without it, our life can become pretty uncomfortable, and we can lose our motivation to meditate. So let's always take adequate time to rest before getting up from deep meditation. Then all of our activities in daily life will be filling up with peace and bliss with minimum disruptions from the inner purification we are undergoing in our deep meditation.

Fine-Tuning Our Meditation Time

For the majority of us, meditating for twenty minutes twice each day will be a good formula for sustaining steady progress over time. Maybe at a later time we will feel the desire to meditate longer. And, for a few of us it will be obvious that twenty minutes is too much. So, this brings up the question of *fine-tuning* our meditation time.

It is important to understand that less can be more in deep meditation and that a lot more can be very much less, to the point of being unhealthy. Inner silence is the most powerful force within us, the power underlying the whole cosmos, and it will transform us over time, taken in balanced amounts on a twice-daily basis.

Imagine driving a car. When we step on the gas, it goes faster. If we are in a hurry, we will step on the gas more. What happens if we come to a curve with a cliff on the outside? Do we keep our foot pressed all the way down on the gas? If we do, oops, over the cliff! Meditation is like that. There is a limit to how much purification our nervous system can tolerate each day, week and month. If we constantly press the gas pedal to the floor with deep meditation, it will not be a good outcome, just like with the car.

What we want to do is find the right balance. To do this we make small adjustments. If we would like to increase our time, we can do so in a five minute increment, and not do it again for at least a few months. Then we will know if we are stable or not with the increased time.

If we are feeling discomfort in activity, even when taking proper rest at the end of deep meditation, we could be meditating too long. This can be so if we are meditating twenty minutes, fifteen minutes, or even less. A few are very sensitive to deep meditation and can achieve the same results with much less time in practice. In that case, we do not go slow in making a downward adjustment in time. If we have too much release and discomfort in daily activity, then we pull back on the time as quickly and as much as necessary to bring things into balance. Once we find a stable time, we should stick with it for a while – weeks at least. If we have pulled back from twenty minutes to ten minutes during a rough patch, and we feel we are over it, then we can inch up five minutes at a time and see how it feels.

This is getting into the very important fine points of regulating our practice for maximum comfort and effectiveness. We call this *self-pacing*. It is the kind of pacing only the individual practitioner can do, and is an important part of navigating the path of inner purification that deep meditation opens up for us.

So, let's always be mindful of how we feel in daily activity after our daily deep meditations, and do the necessary fine-tuning of our time, as necessary. For most of us, it will be none, or very little deviation from twenty minutes. However, for a few, the fine-tuning can be a lot, particularly for those who are very sensitive to deep meditation. In that case, less is definitely more. These instructions are to make sure everyone will have effective means to make the necessary adjustments so the journey can proceed as smoothly as possible. The longer we are involved in doing daily deep meditation, the better we will become at fine-tuning our meditation time. This will be due to the rise of inner silence, which provides us with a much keener sense of the process of inner purification, and how to navigate through it effectively. Self-pacing is a fact of life for all who are involved in spiritual practices. It is an essential skill for practitioners to have at all levels, from beginning to advanced.

Clock-Watching in Meditation

In the first weeks and months of doing twice-daily deep meditation, it is normal to have a bit of a preoccupation with the clock.

It is okay to peek to check the clock once in a while to find our twenty minutes. But we don't need to be checking every minute, or even every five minutes. With more experience, we find that we have a pretty accurate biological clock inside, and we will rarely be off by much if we just rely on that for the majority of our meditation time, checking the physical clock near the end, as necessary.

There is the question about using an alarm of some kind. We definitely don't want to use one that will jar us out of our seat. And it is not best to become dependent on an outside stimulus all the time. Using a soft alarm is okay if we can live without it if we do not have it. That is the point. Sometimes we will have only our watch to confirm the timekeeping of our internal clock.

On a related matter, it is not the end of the world if we fall into one of those sleep-like blackout states discussed earlier, and wake up ten minutes after our time is up. In that case, we just lie down for a little while to make sure we are not carrying unwinding inner purification into our daily activity. If we inadvertently go over on time, it is okay. We just take our rest and get up. But we do not go over on time intentionally. That is not the best practice. We want to be steady in our meditation time over the months and years. Over the long run it will not matter if we slipped a bit here and there. If we have been regular in our practice, and keeping the time reasonably well on balance, we will achieve the desired results with minimum discomfort along the way.

Finding Time to Meditate when "On-the-Go"

Most of us lead busy lives, and that is a blessing. There is no better way to stabilize inner silence gained in deep meditation than to go out and engage fully in activity according to our inclinations.

However, if we are very active, finding the time to meditate can become a challenge. So, this is something we should consider from the beginning when we first learn to meditate. If we do not consider it now, we can get so caught up in life that we can be missing our meditation here and there. And pretty soon we can lose our meditation habit altogether. It can happen to any of us.

So, what is the solution? If we can deeply ingrain our habit of meditation, we will be able to *honor* that wherever we happen to be. In fact, honoring of the practice when it is due each day is developing the habit itself. This does not mean we will close our eyes and meditate in the middle of a meeting. But it does mean that we can meditate on the airplane, on the train, while sitting waiting for an appointment, or for a few minutes before our dinner break while working on a project deadline. Even if we only sit for a few minutes on a bench on a busy street with eyes closed, easily picking up our mantra, we have honored the habit of meditation. This honoring sustains our habit, so we will always be able to take the time we have to continue our daily deep meditation.

Sometimes we will have little time to meditate. Other times we will have plenty of time. Either way, we can sustain our habit by closing our eyes. That is the key. As long as we find the urge to meditate wherever we are at the appointed time, and acknowledge it in some way, however small, we will be on the path.

Of course, if we are living way out of balance in terms of daily activity, it will catch up with us sooner or later. In that case, establishing and keeping a deep meditation habit will be very difficult. The chances are that a routine of excessive activity will disrupt other areas of our life as well. In that case, maybe we should step back and assess our overall situation. If we are never finding the time to meditate, we are probably not finding the time for other important aspects of our life either. Bringing our life in balance has great value. Short term circumstances may not always favor a balanced life, but if we have not moved toward balance over the long run, then it may be time to take a closer look at how we are living. Beginning and sustaining a daily deep meditation routine is a good way to get the ball rolling in the right direction. Reducing mental activity on a scheduled basis can bring much more happiness into our life in the form of blissful inner silence. Then when we are very active, we will be cradled in our stillness at the same time, and our choices will naturally gravitate toward more balance in life.

Meditating After Meals or at Bedtime

With a busy schedule, we may find ourselves with few alternatives for doing our deep meditation each day. It may be that the only time we will have available sometimes will be right after a meal, or right before bedtime.

There are specific reasons why this is not the best approach. Because deep meditation reduces our body functions and overall metabolism, it will be going in the opposite direction from any activity that is coming up in the body, like digestion. So it will be good to wait at least an hour after a meal before meditating.

Because deep meditation is a preparation for activity, it can keep us awake if we do it right before bedtime. So it is recommended that we meditate at least an hour before bedtime and have at least a little activity between meditation and going to bed.

Having said those things about meals and bedtime, it is possible that some of us will not be so affected by the factors just mentioned. It may be that for some of us, meditating after a meal or right before bedtime will not cause any difficulty. We will only know if we try and see. Even the worst case will not be a disaster (some indigestion or some lost sleep), and it is good to know how we will react doing our meditation in different circumstances. Not that we should make a habit of meditating right after dinner or right before bed. No. But we may not have a choice and we will no doubt have the opportunity to run the experiment on ourselves sometime. That's okay. We need to find out what our options are.

Hopefully, we will be able to keep a steady routine of deep meditation before morning and evening meals, with good activity during the day and evening, and normal sleep at night. And for those times when we are in a pinch, we will know what works for us and what does not. Our own experience will be the best indicator of what we can do to keep up our practice.

Alcohol, Tobacco and Drugs

As we know, deep meditation stimulates a process of purification deep within our nervous system. Meditation is a very fine tool for deep cleaning, but not necessarily the best one to use for clearing out recently ingested substances like alcohol, tobacco or recreational drugs. Because these substances act directly on the brain and affect our mental acuity, it is not in our best interest to have them in our system during deep meditation, or even within days of practicing deep meditation. If we do, the results of our meditation will not be optimal.

If we have had some non-addicted reliance on substances, and are able to get started with regular deep meditation, we will find that our interest in such things will naturally tend to fall off. This is because we will feel the rise of inner silence coming up from within. When that kind of joy is coming up, we will feel less drawn to the chemical additives that we have used in the past to try and temporarily replace the real thing we are naturally experiencing now within us with deep meditation.

At the same time, it is unreasonable to expect that deep meditation alone can cure us of a deep-rooted dependency on alcohol, tobacco or drugs. For that, we will need the help of a good program designed specifically for such things. *The Twelve Step Program* is ideal for this and has been adapted to accommodate many kinds of dependencies.

If we can reduce or eliminate our intake of substances that interfere with our attention and awareness, then meditation will have a good chance to carry us the rest of the way.

Imagine a window with lots of dirt on it. We'd like to clean the window so we can fully enjoy the sunshine coming in from outside. With meditation, we can clean the window to the finest degree. But can we clean the window if someone is throwing shovels full of mud on the window every day? It will be more than our fine meditation tool can overcome. Somehow we must stop the mud from being thrown on the window so we can move on with the very fine cleaning of meditation that will enable us to see the sun in its full glory.

In the case of a drug prescribed by our doctor for a medical condition, it is a different story. We should respect the advice of our doctor. If we think a prescribed drug is interfering with our ability to practice deep meditation, then we should talk with our doctor to see if there is something that can be worked out that will be for the benefit of our health, and also in support of our desire to meditate.

Diet

It is not necessary to make any special diet changes when we begin deep meditation. Whatever we are comfortable eating will be fine to continue with.

As we advance in our experience we may find that our body is *talking* to us about what we put in it in the way of food. And we will have a more sensitive ear to listen to our body, so we will hear it better than we did before. The result of this communication from our body and our hearing it may lead to some different choices we make about our diet.

So, while there is no diet guidance being offered here relating to deep meditation, many of us may find ourselves leaning toward a lighter, more nutritious diet. This is not a bad thing. It is well known that lighter, fresher foods bring better health. But we don't have to be deciding anything about it at the beginning. Deep meditation will naturally increase our awareness about diet and other things that will be more in line with the inner purification going on in our nervous system and maintaining good health. The choices we make will be our choices, and will be made in our own best interest as we progress along the path toward more peace, creativity and personal freedom.

Physical Exercise and Culture

We already know that when we sit to meditate, our body functions settle down. There is great power in this to heal and purify us mentally, emotionally and physically. That is the mind/body connection working for our benefit in a practical way through daily deep meditation practice.

Anyone who has engaged in physical exercise knows that the mind/body connection goes the other way too. In fact, in addition to maintaining physical health, physical exercise is a primary means used by many people to maintain mental and emotional health also. Whether we are engaged in muscle-toning, aerobic exercise, martial arts, or yoga postures, we are there in large part for the mental and emotional benefits that come with conditioning of the body.

Can we benefit by engaging in a program of physical culture in addition to our daily deep meditation? Absolutely. If we take things in proper balance, there is much that can be gained. Paradoxically, the stillness we gain in deep meditation can lead to profound levels of physical conditioning when we are active. And the physical exercise we engage in can help lead to more profound levels of inner silence being cultivated in deep meditation. So, in keeping with the mind/body connection, a program of deep meditation and a program of physical conditioning provide much greater benefits than doing only one of these alone.

What kind of physical conditioning is best, and when should we do it in relation to our meditation sessions?

The goal here is not to rearrange our current life and activities to suit someone's perception of what the ideal program of physical culture is. If we have an exercise program already that works, we can keep it. If we do not have one, well, this book is not needed to point to the benefits that regular exercise can bring. What we can advise on here is *when* physical exercise is best done in relation to our deep meditation sessions. It is simple enough.

The best time to engage in physical exercise of the athletic variety is *after* our deep meditation session. That means after our complete practice, including taking adequate rest before getting up. So, then, after our normal warm-up, we can engage fully in our athletic physical activity, whatever it may be. As we have said, deep meditation is a preparation for activity.

Due to scheduling considerations, if we are inclined to engage in strenuous physical exercise before deep meditation, we should allow time to cool down before sitting to meditate. We would normally do that anyway before resuming our day's activities, yes? – Coming off intense physical activity slowly, taking a shower, relaxing for a while, etc. So that would be okay before sitting for deep meditation also.

In the case of yoga postures, we are talking about two categories of physical activity. These days, yoga postures are often done as fitness-style physical exercise, even to the point of being aerobic, meaning elevating the metabolism in an exercise mode. This type of yoga posture practice is beneficial as physical exercise, and should be done after deep meditation, or well before it, just as we would do for any exercise of the athletic variety.

Then there are yoga postures in the traditional way, which are slow and easy bending and stretching exercises that are designed to open up our nervous system inside for a smoother flow of our inner energies. Traditional yoga postures also help cultivate our inner stillness. So there is a connection here with deep meditation. The application of traditional yoga postures in relation to deep meditation is different from more strenuous forms of physical culture.

With traditional yoga postures, we find a complimentary practice that can directly support our deep meditation. Yoga postures of this kind we can do *right before* our deep meditation sitting. They can help us settle down before we meditate, smoothing some of the rough physical edges, so to speak, before we dive deep with the mind in our meditation session.

So if we have been doing traditional yoga postures, it will be very good to do a short routine right before our deep meditation session, if we would like to do that. Other forms of exercise that are more strenuous we can benefit from also, and these should be done after deep meditation, or well before, so as not to have too much activity coming into our meditation session.

Self-Pacing Versus Breaking Through

With some things, the harder we push, the faster we can progress, with no apparent limit. With those things, if we push hard enough, we can *break through*. There is a lot we can do with practices to enhance our spiritual progress, but in this special arena of purifying and opening our nervous system, there are limits to how fast we can go while maintaining stability at the same time. Without stability in our deep meditation practice and our daily life, we cannot sustain practice for very long. None of us likes to keep hitting ourselves in the head with a hammer. If we are inclined toward excess in our practice, deep meditation can be like that.

Growing with deep meditation is more like cultivating a plant. If we keep it watered and fertilized in the right amount, in its own time it will grow to be strong and healthy. If we over-water it and put on too much fertilizer – well, you know what happens. Managing a program of daily deep meditation is like that. Everyone will be a bit different in this, as was discussed when we talked about fine-tuning our meditation time. Once we have optimized our practice and made it our own, we will have found the right blend that suits our growth just right. We call this *self-pacing*. With good self-pacing, we can go on independently with great success over the long term.

On the other hand, if we are inclined to meditate twenty minutes one day, two hours the next day and not at all the next, we will be inviting less-than-satisfactory progress, and probably quite a bit of instability in our life as well.

So, keep in mind that pushing hard with the aim of breaking through is not the preferred strategy when considering taking up deep meditation. And neither is inconsistency in our daily practice routine. Less can be more with our daily deep meditation practice. The journey is not a sprint. It is a marathon. As with the tortoise and the hare, slow and steady will reach the finish line first.

So let's keep self-pacing in mind as we navigate through our twice-daily deep meditation practice over the weeks, months and years.

Effects in Daily Activity

We become used to the benefits of deep meditation very quickly. The qualities of peace, creativity and energy that come to be part of our everyday life as inner silence comes up are so natural that we may barely notice. Happiness is our natural condition. It is often only when we are less than happy that we will notice something is amiss.

For that reason, it is not uncommon for others to notice a change in us after we have been meditating a few days or weeks, before we may notice anything ourselves. So often, new meditators hear it from their family, friends and coworkers. "You seem so calm." "You haven't lost your temper in weeks. What's going on?" "You are smiling more lately." And so on... While others are noticing the improvement in our demeanor, we may not. We are just living it, with a gradually growing inner smile.

Or we may be going along with our meditations and our daily life, only to realize months later that we are seeing the world differently than we did before. That could be triggered by an experience where we do not react as fearfully as we may have during similar experiences in the past. It is over time that we will notice the most change in ourselves. Then it becomes clear that we are not operating the same way that we used to. And that is a good thing.

The path of unfoldment that we travel with deep meditation is a long one with profound long term possibilities. Yet, we can begin to enjoy the benefits right away as soon as we begin practice. And so can those around us, which is the greatest gift we can give to the world. By traveling a path to personal freedom for ourselves, we are traveling it for everyone else too.

Visions and Energy Experiences

There are other kinds of experiences we can have during or after our deep meditation sessions. We might even have them before we have learned to meditate. Such experiences are clear inner or outer perceptions that we could call *visions* or *energy movements*. When they happen in our meditation practice, they will always be symptoms of purification, with something added beyond the ordinary thoughts, feelings and sensations we have. When they happen outside our meditation, they will be what have been called *psychic*, *extrasensory* or *mystical* experiences.

Whatever we choose to call these experiences, they can happen both inside and outside deep meditation. The question many will ask is, "What are these experiences and how do they relate to my meditation practice and my life?"

We will review several categories of this kind of experience, and see how these are handled as we navigate along our path of daily deep meditation practice.

Inner Sights and Sounds

Our sensory faculties are multi-dimensional. We often take for granted that we have the ability to perceive wavelengths of light, sound vibrations in the air, and other ranges of energy and chemical characteristics with our five senses. Yet, we may be surprised when we suddenly experience something beyond the range of our normal sensory inputs. That gets our attention. At least in the beginning it does. Later on, we might not even notice that we are perceiving the world in a way that we could not have imagined before. It is easy to get used to improved perception, just as it is easy to get used to rising inner silence and the happiness it brings.

As inner silence comes up in our nervous system, it is possible that we will have some new sensory experiences within our nervous system – inner lights, sounds, touches, tastes and smells. They can be very subtle, or very noticeable.

If such inner sensory experiences happen during our meditation, we will be wise to regard them like any other experience we have, and just easily come back to our mantra. It is important to understand that experiences we have in meditation, no matter how profound, are only byproducts of the process of inner purification we are engaged in. They are the *scenery* we see along the way on our journey. As soon as we go intentionally off into those experiences, we are no longer meditating. The experiences themselves are not the practice. They are the result of the practice. So, if we are steady in our deep meditation, following the simple procedure of easily coming back to the mantra when we realize we are off it, we will be cultivating more inner silence, and our perception of our inner and outer dimensions will gradually expand.

If we are having such experiences outside our meditations, then we can enjoy them according to our own inclinations. Eventually we will see all of the world for what it is – an endless flow of radiating interconnected energy, and an expression of our own inner nature, which is blissful stillness. So, the natural expansion of our inner sensuality is also an expansion of our perception of the world.

As long as we are favoring our deep meditation practice when we are sitting for it, our view of ourselves and the world will continue to deepen and expand. Inner sensory experiences are a natural expression of our growth, and we will be wise to regard them as we do any other sensory stimuli during our deep meditation sessions.

Sensations of Energy Flowing Inside

There are two basic levels of experience within us. The first is *inner silence*, our most fundamental form of awareness, which is the foundation of what we are and all that is around us. The second is *energy* – all that is manifest, which we experience and perceive with our senses.

When inner silence is stimulated to a greater presence, the energy that flows out from it is also stimulated. It is a paradox that inner silence (profound stillness) leads to more dynamic activity. Yet, that is what we will experience on many levels as we progress with our deep meditation practice.

So, it will not be unusual if we feel sensations of energy moving within us. It is part of the purification process and is, in fact, what is behind the thoughts, feelings and sensations we are having during deep meditation.

Such movements of inner energy in our nervous system can also be experienced in more exotic ways, and with greater intensity. There can be sensory qualities involved, as discussed previously. The distinction between an inner sensory experience and an outright energy experience will be in the intensity. With an energy experience, we can feel the physical quality of it coursing through our nervous system. We may feel heat, physical pressure, shivers, prickly sensations, or goose bumps. There can be elation, a quickening of breath (panting), or involuntary laughter or crying. There can also be symptoms that are similar to various yoga practices, such as the eyes going up, the tongue going back on the roof of our mouth, head movements, and so on. If any of these things happen, there is nothing to be alarmed about. It is purification, just more *scenery* on our journey.

We treat energy experiences the same way we do any other experience that may come up in meditation

– when we realize our attention has gone off the mantra, we easily come back to it.

If we find that energy experiences become excessive while we are meditating, we can back off from the mantra and just take it easy for a few minutes. If the sensations continue to be strong, we can lie down for a while until they subside, counting that as part of our meditation time. And remember, we always rest at the end of our meditation before we get up.

If we experience such symptoms during our daily activity, and they become excessive with no sign of subsiding, we should consider reducing our time of meditation for a few days or weeks until things settle down, as we discussed earlier on fine-tuning our meditation time. Once our inner energies have stabilized in daily activity, we can consider inching our time back up, five minutes at a time.

All energy sensations are symptoms of purification occurring in our nervous system. The sensations are caused by the *friction* of neurobiological energy flowing through subtle nerves that are not yet fully purified. The more energy there is, and the less purified the nerves, the more the energy sensations will be. So we want to regulate the amount of energy that is stimulated so it is just enough to purify our nervous system, but not so much to be causing too much disruption. As our subtle nerves gradually become purified, they can handle much more energy with far less resistance. That is when our experiences will go from the coarser types of energy symptoms to having more of the quality of ecstasy. Same energy. Same neurology. Ultimately, more flow with less resistance and steadily increasing ecstasy.

If we are aware of the dynamics of this process of purification, we will be in a much better position to regulate our deep meditation practice accordingly, and will have a lot less concern about it, because we will know what is going on and how to navigate through it.

Sexual Arousal

One of the manifestations of energy movement in our nervous system can come in the form of sexual arousal. It can happen from time to time, and is normal. There is a close relationship between our sexuality and the course of our spiritual progress. The energy coming up from our sexual biology will gradually expand through our nervous system as we advance on our spiritual path. Deep meditation alone can stimulate this process. Some arousal can happen as our sexual biology responds to new levels of stimulation from the rise of inner silence. Later on, there will be much more energy flowing up through us with little or no external symptoms of sexuality being involved. When sexual energy is going to that higher purpose in the neurobiology, we call it *spiritual energy*.

If sexual arousal occurs in meditation, we follow the same guidelines as when any other experience is happening. We always easily favor the mantra.

The expansion of our sexual function to a spiritual purpose does not take away our ability to engage in sexual relations, or our ability to have children. It is an expansion of sexual function to more purpose, not giving up one neurobiological function (reproduction) to gain another neurobiological function (enlightenment). We are capable of being fully functional in both realms.

Premonitions, Clairvoyance and Clairaudience

We all have latent abilities that may be manifesting to a lesser or greater degree. Some people are born with remarkable *gifts* for sensing future events, spiritual energies, non-physical beings, and similar phenomena. The world is full of evidence of these things.

If we are practicing deep meditation, we may notice our ability for having these kinds of perceptions increasing somewhat. After all, if our inner silence is rising and our inner sensory abilities are opening, it stands to reason that we will see more of what is there that we may not have seen before. There is nothing to be alarmed about in this. In fact, at the same time that our sensory perception is deepening, we will also be attracting benevolent energies much more, and chaotic energies much less. So, along with refinements in perception, we also will be seeing much more of the positive in life. Rising inner silence brings us both.

The gifts that come to us in this way will be a part of our increasing ability to help others, and we will be able to do so without even thinking about it. In other words, we do not develop an ability and then go out and look for people to help with the ability. No. We develop ourselves spiritually in the broadest sense by cultivating pure bliss consciousness in our nervous system, and then we find ourselves much more inclined to help others. Then the means that are necessary to support that service to others will come to us also. So the process of unfoldment and the manifestation of divine power is not so much on the basis of our detailed choices. We do choose, but it is from the level of our consciousness, our inner silence. That which we are cultivating within in deep meditation is all peace, love and benevolence. Through deep meditation, we gradually become a channel for the qualities of inner silence and the gifts that come with that. In doing so we come to live a life in freedom, ecstatic bliss and loving service.

If we are having premonitions or other clairvoyant experiences during our deep meditation session, we will be wise to just easily favor our mantra when we realize we are off it. The visions will be there later if they are needed in our life for some reason. If they are coming randomly in daily activity for no apparent reason, then we will be wise to just let them go, understanding that we are engaged in a long term process of purification and opening.

When we are in deep meditation mode, all of these experiences are aspects of the process of purification we are engaged in, and should be regarded accordingly.

Visions of Religious Figures

If we are sitting in meditation and the divine inspiration of our religion comes riding up to us in a golden chariot, what shall we do? If it is Jesus, or Buddha, or Krishna, or Moses, or Mohammed, and they ask us to go for a ride in their golden chariot with them, what shall we do?

It is very simple. We easily go back to our mantra at whatever level in the mind we may be.

You might ask, "How can we favor our mantra over one of those great saviors of humanity? Is the mantra greater than they are?"

It is not that we are favoring the mantra over the great ones. We are meditating. And when we are meditating, we are favoring the mantra over everything that comes up, so that we can know all things at the deepest level of truth by cultivating our pure bliss consciousness. By doing this, we will know the great ones much better. We will know the truth in our own religion better than we did before. So, the simple procedure we do in deep meditation is not a case of making a value judgment about anything. It is just a procedure that will deepen our perception and appreciation of everything. Once we are finished with our meditation session, our savoir will still be there with us, and all the brighter in our vision, due to our inner cultivation of pure bliss consciousness.

Didn't the great ones all say the same thing? "Know yourself and you will know God."

"Discover the light within and you will know my light."

"Seek first the kingdom of heaven and all will be added to you."

That is what we are doing with this simple procedure called deep meditation.

Practice Versus the Sirens of Spiritual Experience

By now, we can see the benefit of forming a habit for how we regard all that we may see happening in our deep meditation sessions. And that is to always come back to the mantra when we remember that we have been off it, no matter what the experience may be. The only exception we have noted here is in the case where excessive purification is occurring that is uncomfortable to the point where we cannot easily pick up the mantra. Then we use the procedures that have been described for that. Also, obviously, if someone yells, "Fire!" or there is any other physical emergency, we should do whatever is necessary to protect life and limb.

It is fairly easy to let go of random streams of thoughts in deep meditation, or the routine sorts of emotions and physical sensations that can happen. But when we are having glamorous visions and ecstatic energy experiences in deep meditation, there can be that temptation to take the ride. If we do, we will be off of our meditation procedure, and our results will vary accordingly. So, we can regard such glamorous experiences in meditation as *sirens* that can distract us from what we are doing. When we see these things in our deep meditation sessions, it will be good to remember that it is the practice that will bring us home, not any particular experience we might be tempted to give our attention to while we are sitting there.

For the rest, if we are following the correct procedure in our meditations, we will find gradual improvements on many fronts in our daily life – less stress, better health, more inner peace, more creativity, more enthusiasm, and more love and compassion for others. And, who knows? Maybe a divine savior will offer us a ride in their golden chariot sometime. For the glamorous things we let go of in favor of the mantra in deep meditation, there will always be an opportunity later on.

As long as we are on the path, there will always be more for us to see and do. Each day will bring more freedom.

The Rise of Inner Silence – The Witness

We have talked about *inner silence*, particularly from the viewpoint of cultivating it in deep meditation – traveling the path of inner purification. Now we will look at it more from the side of experiences in our daily activity.

This is not a philosophy we are espousing here. In scriptures and philosophical treatises we can read long dissertations on the nature of consciousness and the nature of life. The mind can try to grasp all this, and what will it mean? Not much. We can't know what an apple tastes like until we bite into one. It is that simple.

The proof of the pudding is not in looking at it, but in eating it!

Discussions about consciousness are only that – discussions. So let us resolve to stick with discussions of *real experiences* here, not theories. If it is described in this book, and you can't go out and experience it as a result of your own deep meditation practice, then you are not obligated to believe any of this. Experience is the final arbiter of what is true and what is not. You don't have to take anyone else's word for it. The practice of deep meditation is both self-directed and self-validating.

By now, you might already have a feel for what the rise of inner silence is like. Perhaps you have been meditating for a few days and have had a taste of it. Or maybe you are coming back to this book for a review after a few months of daily deep meditation and can feel the quality of inner stillness in this very moment.

There are several ways we can notice our rising inner silence. That is, if others haven't noticed something going on in us first, and said something to us about it.

There can be a general sense of peace, a slight euphoric feeling that seems to be following us around all day. We might find ourselves shrinking a bit less from the challenges that we face each day, and participating more in discussions where we felt we did not have much to offer before. Or maybe we just feel like taking on more in life – with a new found energy we have. The signs of rising inner silence are endless. But there is one symptom that is unmistakable, and this is the emergence of *the witness*.

What on earth is "the witness?" Is it some divine being that creeps up from within us? It sounds a bit like science fiction, doesn't it? The invasion of the witness or something like that.

Well, it could be kind of scary, except for one simple fact. The witness is *our own self* in the deepest sense. It is that part of us that experiences everything we are aware of – our thoughts, our feelings, our physical sensations, the world around us. Everything. Let all that fade away and what we are left with is the witness, our own special self, which does not move or change throughout all the experiences we have in our entire life. That is what we are cultivating in deep meditation.

Isn't it true that there is a part of you that has not changed one iota since you were a little child? Perhaps you miss the innocence of that sweet joyful awareness you had as a child, which has been covered by layers and layers of experiences in the world, and the lingering impressions from all that stuff. Wouldn't it be nice to recover that sweet awareness without having to entirely give up your current adult life? After all, being an adult does have its advantages. We can do this. That is what deep meditation is all about. Recovering the freedom of innocent awareness in our daily life, without having to change our preferred lifestyle to do it.

Noticing our witness for the first time is a revelation. Not that we have to realize anything. One day we will just notice that while something happened we were watching it from a quiet place inside that is not touched. Or we will be doing something and notice that the greater part of us is not in the doing, but quietly watching, untouched, and perhaps even smiling a bit on the inside. That is what it is like.

The witness is a feeling of separation from the humdrum of the world. A cozy place that we can call *our self.* It will be the most noticeable in the midst of activity. That is when the contrast between our inner self and the world will be most pronounced. Even those who do not meditate tend to witness themselves when there is total chaos going on. Life becomes like a dream in that situation. For the long-time meditator, life surely is like a dream – a joyful dream, even in the worst of external circumstances.

One might argue that to be in such a condition would be inappropriate, irresponsible and downright uncaring. That is one of the mysteries of the spiritual growth that occurs with the rise of inner silence and the witness. While we are becoming more joyful, less overwhelmed and more free from the travails of the world, we also become much more engaged, more compassionate and far more able to aid ourselves and others in the most trying of circumstances.

This is the miracle of the rise of inner silence and the witness. At the same time that we are becoming free, we are also able to give more to the world than we ever could before. And the more we do that, the freer we become.

Stillness in Action

There can be no doubt that the growth of spiritual life is a paradox. Stillness in action? What could be more a paradox than that? Yet, that is what happens with the rise of inner silence. In time it becomes normal for us. We can smile while the building is falling down, even as we are saving everyone in it. Divine consciousness is capable of doing things like that. It is stillness in action. Enlightenment is at its best in the best of times, and it is also at its best in the worst of times.

Does this mean we will not grieve at the loss of a loved one? It does not mean that. We will have the same feelings and sensitivities we had before. We will cry at weddings and funerals like we did before – perhaps even more than we did before, because we will *feel* everything much deeper inside ourselves. But we will not suffer. Our roots will be beyond suffering. Everyone feels pain. But suffering is only for those who have become identified with their pain. With the rise of inner silence and the witness, we will still feel pain, but we will not become our pain and we will suffer no more. That is the difference. That is how freedom works.

There is no escape from life. As we evolve, we will become life itself, feeling it in the deepest reaches of our soul. At the same time, the joys and sorrows of this world will be but waves on our great unmoving sea of pure bliss consciousness.

But, for now, we'd be happy to navigate through the day a little better, yes? … On our way to realizing ourselves as the great infinite sea of life. Not to worry, there is plenty of room for active participation and fruitful results every step along the way, from the day we sit to meditate for the first time.

So, whatever amount of stillness we have, whether we have been meditating for one day, one thousand days, or ten thousand days, it is incumbent on us to go out and be active. Stillness does not want to stand still! It wants to move and express itself in the world.

That is the deal, see? In exchange for this wonderful liberating inner silence we are cultivating in deep meditation, we are obliged to go out and do something with it in the world. Who decides what we are to do in the world with our inner silence? We do. It is according to our own inclinations that we go out and engage in our daily activities. But there is an interesting angle in this. As we are becoming more infused with our inner silence, our own inner self, we are also making our choices in life from a deeper level within ourselves. They are still our choices, but coming from a much wiser place within us. So, we will find our choices in life gradually shifting to be more in line with our long term wellbeing and the wellbeing of those around us. Our same thought streams will be seen by us from a much deeper level, and our choices will contain more wisdom. Wisdom comes from inner silence.

This is why we say, meditate and then go out and be active in the world. By this we are engaging our inner silence in our daily thoughts, words and deeds, facilitating the growth and stabilization of inner silence, the witness, in our nervous system and ongoing experience of life.

So the path of deep meditation is two-fold. Through the simple procedure of meditation, we dive within to our pure bliss consciousness. Then we come out and engage in our daily activities in the world, which stabilizes the quality of inner silence in us. This two-fold process leads to the rise of our inner silence and the phenomenon of *stillness in action.*

Chapter 4 – Freedom

It has been said that freedom is a state of mind. What creates a state of mind that is free? What is the underlying cause of freedom? We can call it a state of *being*.

Beyond our thoughts and feelings is something unshakable that can illuminate us like nothing in the external world can. When we are illuminated in this way, we are not only free in our external surroundings, whatever they may be, we are also free within ourselves – free in the face of all our thoughts, feelings and physical sensations. This brings us blissfully into what has been called *the now*, where our happiness no longer depends on a particular flow of events, including our memories of the past or our desires for the future. We are happy in the present with whatever is happening, with whatever we are doing, and are able to act without prejudices that do not belong to the moment at hand. This does not mean we will not have a vision for our life or for the world. We can choose our vision, whatever it is we are inclined to work for. But it will not own us. We will be living and working always in the present.

Through deep meditation, we will know that our being is stillness. Not as an idea or a concept. But as a direct experience. Inner stillness is a natural ability we all have, a condition that can be invited without a monumental effort. All human beings are destined to know themselves as inner silence and, therefore, all are destined to be free. We each know this deep in our heart. Our personal freedom is as near as our willingness to act on our own desire. We can have it simply by going within each day.

And there is more. Not only is our personal freedom cultivated in deep meditation in the form of unshakable inner silence … In addition, in meditation the seeds are sown for our evolution toward unending ecstatic bliss and divine love expanding outward from within us. These developments constitute a full flowering of enlightenment that reaches far beyond the boundaries of our physical body.

Unshakable Inner Silence and Ecstasy

We have spoken of the rise of inner silence in our twice-daily practice of deep meditation, which is stabilized through our normal daily activities. As inner silence becomes more pervasive in our nervous system, we will at some point notice the witness quality. This is the part of us that is not impacted or changed by events, including everything happening in our external environment and everything in our internal environment. As inner silence becomes our steady state condition, we will have personal freedom. Then our nature, our sense of self, can be described simply as permanent *unshakable inner silence*.

The qualities of this condition are peace, creativity, flexibility, strength, steadfastness and love. Permeating all of these qualities is something we can call *bliss* – a quiet happiness that never goes away. And it too is unshakable, like everything else we naturally radiate from within our unshakable inner silence.

If that were all that we gained from practicing deep meditation over the long term, it would seem like plenty, yes? Yet, there is more – much more.

Unshakable inner silence, in all of its pristine glory, is but the first milestone in what we call the overall process of *human spiritual transformation.* There are additional milestones of development that we will find naturally emerging in our nervous system and everyday experiences.

Somewhere along the way on our journey with deep meditation and the purification and opening that occurs within us, we will experience what can be described as *ecstasy*. In contrast to bliss, which is an inseparable aspect of our inner silence, ecstasy is a symptom of inner energy moving through our purifying nervous system. This energy is called *prana* – also known as our *life-force*. It is the movement of prana within us that animates our physical, mental and emotional existence, and all that exists in our surroundings, as well.

Deep meditation influences the prana within us, enlivening it on the level of our inner silence. It is the movement of prana that we experience in the form of thoughts, feelings and physical sensation as our nervous system goes through the cycles of purification during our meditation sessions. As purification advances, the movement of prana through our nerves will produce increasing pleasure, or ecstatic sensations. This is a normal consequence of our nervous system being purified deep within.

There are additional means that can be applied to cultivate our ability to conduct more prana throughout our nervous system, giving rise to increasing levels of divine ecstasy. These additional means include specific practices involving mind (samyama), breath (pranayama), body (asanas, mudras and bandhas), and sexuality (tantra). These additional methods are covered in other volumes listed on the last page of this book.

The question may arise, why do we need to be cultivating ecstasy on top of inner silence? Isn't inner silence enough? Inner silence may be enough for us, but remaining in stillness is not enough for our inner silence!

Once inner silence is resident within us, it is natural for it to stimulate prana into greater expression in our nervous system. We first experience this through the symptoms of purification we have discussed. Then it will be crossing over into ecstatic experiences through a natural progression of the pranic energy moving within us. The additional practices mentioned help cultivate and balance this process, which will likely be initiated and going on anyway from the results of our deep meditation alone. So the additional methods are there to aid in cultivating a smooth and balanced manifestation of prana.

Ecstasy itself is an interim step to what is a far greater outcome. By cultivating the expression of both inner silence and beneficial flow of prana in our nervous system, we will be setting the stage for ever greater manifestations of the vast potential for happiness and good which lies within us all.

Refinement to Ecstatic Bliss

If ecstasy is an interim step on the way to more, what will that "more" be?

We know that *bliss* is an inherent quality of the inner silence we cultivate in deep meditation. In other words, bliss is not a quality we cultivate by itself as something dynamic within us. It comes with the package of inner silence, so to speak. It is a built-in aspect of pure bliss consciousness. It is what we have when we remove the obstructions in our nervous system.

On the other hand, *ecstasy* is a product of energy movement within us – the movement of prana through our nerves. In its early stages, ecstasy is very much a by-product of the process of purification going on inside. It can, in fact, be trumped up quite a lot by the *friction* of prana racing through our partially-purified nerves. As our nervous system opens over time, and becomes a better conductor of prana (and ecstasy), then something amazing happens – a remarkable refinement.

Over time, the line between ecstasy and bliss will become blurred. There is a gradual blending of these two qualities. Or, to put it more succinctly, there is a merging of ecstasy and inner silence. The two become one, and we can call that one, *ecstatic bliss*. Experientially, it is the joining of body and spirit. This is a long process of merging taking place over many months and years. In a sense, it begins the first time we sit in deep meditation, and continues for our entire career of doing deep meditation and other practices we may undertake along the way to aid our progress.

One thing we can be sure of is that, with continuing practices over time, ecstasy will refine, the presence of inner silence (and its qualities) will become steadfast, and ecstatic bliss will result – a condition of unending vibrating stillness which we know as our self.

This is good to know, because ecstasy can be rather extreme in its early stages, and an occasional distraction from our practice. As purification proceeds, it refines. The end result bears little resemblance to the rough-and-tumble forms of ecstasy we may experience in the early stages.

What do we gain as ecstasy refines and inner silence stabilizes? In the various traditions around the world, this joining of inner silence and ecstasy in the human being has been called a *divine union* that yields a *divine birth* within the human being. The birth of a new dynamic within us. It is the dynamic of *divine love*.

Expansion of Divine Love in the World

The changes we are discussing here are based on a neurobiological process of transformation that occurs in the human nervous system. This is directly observable by anyone who engages in deep meditation and the additional practices that promote the changes. We can each verify the outcome for ourselves.

We have indicated that one of the characteristics of rising inner silence in our life is *love*, which will be readily observable in the form of increasing empathy and compassion for others. The longer we have been meditating, the more important the wellbeing of others will become to us. Why is this? It is because we see more and more of our self in the world around us, and act accordingly.

There is a flow involved in the rise of compassion in us. We can call it the flow of consciousness – an unending march toward realization of the unity in all things. As we continue with our daily deep meditation, we become more aware of the oneness of all things.

The merging of inner silence and ecstatic energies within us takes this process to a new level. Once our ecstatic nature has settled into the stillness of our pure bliss consciousness, then we begin to experience a new dynamic. While we are free in our unshakable inner silence, the intimate joining of inner silence and ecstasy that has occurred in us beckons us outward again. An awakened nervous system pulsating in silence expands in all directions. It is a boiling over of love. This is not a boiling over of sentimentality, though we will certainly be sentimental enough due to our greatly deepened sensitivity for all of life. But this overflowing also contains the qualities of pure bliss consciousness – peace, creativity, steadfastness, compassion and so on.

It is an overflowing of inner silence through us into the surroundings. It will happen if we are doing nothing but sitting there. More than likely we will do more than sit, especially if our normal inclination is to be active. We will follow our ecstatic bliss out into the world in the form of service to others. This is not a moral guideline. It is just what happens when we become free within ourselves, and merged in heart, mind, body and spirit. We become a pure channel for the expansion of divine love.

This expansion is a new beginning, a new stage in the process. We realize that our own freedom is but a stepping stone in the grand scheme of nature. We will be inclined to go onward until all human beings are able to experience freedom also. Their freedom is a maturing of our own freedom. And so goes the influence of inner silence, ever outward without limit.

Freedom is a multi-dimensional phenomenon that begins with the establishment of our individual freedom in inner silence, and then moves on through to the maturation of ecstatic bliss in us, which then moves out to encompass everyone in the form of loving service – expansion of divine love.

One of the primary means for traveling the road to freedom is deep meditation. It is a simple practice we can do to achieve practical results in our daily life, while at the same time contributing to the rising freedom of every human being on the earth.

Further Reading and Support

Yogani is an American spiritual scientist who, for more than thirty years, has been integrating ancient techniques from around the world which cultivate human spiritual transformation. The approach he has developed is non-sectarian, and open to all. In the order published, his books include:

Advanced Yoga Practices – Easy Lessons for Ecstatic Living
A large user-friendly textbook providing 240 detailed lessons on the AYP integrated system of advanced yoga practices.

The Secrets of Wilder – A Novel
The story of young Americans discovering and utilizing actual secret practices leading to human spiritual transformation.

The AYP Enlightenment Series
Easy-to-read instruction books on yoga practices, including:

Deep Meditation – Pathway to Personal Freedom

Spinal Breathing Pranayama – Journey to Inner Space
(Due out spring 2006)

Tantra – Discovering the Power of Pre-Orgasmic Sex
(Due out spring 2006)

Asanas, Mudras and Bandhas – Secrets of Inner Ecstasy
(Due out second half 2006)

Samyama – Manifesting the Power of Inner Silence
(Due out second half 2006)

Additional *AYP Enlightenment Series* books are planned…

For up-to-date information on the writings of Yogani, and for the free *AYP Support Forums*, please visit:

www.advancedyogapractices.com

Printed in the United States
48928LVS00001BA/179